Ask, Listen and Grow

A Guide to Active Listening for Enhanced Communication

Table of Contents

Chapter 1. Introduction

Welcome to an exciting journey that promises to revolutionize your communication! In our Special Report, "Ask, Listen, and Grow: A Guide to Active Listening for Enhanced Communication," we'll enlighten you on the transformative power of truly hearing and understanding others. This insightful guide keeps things lighthearted and digestible, while offering invaluable advice on practicing active listening, the secret ingredient that can supercharge your personal and professional relationships. Look forward to success stories, practical exercises, and expert insights that motivate and equip you to redefine communication as you know it. So why wait? Dive in and unfold the charm of listening, understanding, and growing. Your journey towards becoming a communication connoisseur starts the moment you get your hands on this indispensable report!

Chapter 2. The Power of Active Listening

The transformative power of listening has been grandly understated, especially in a world where everyone seems to be focused on putting their ideas forward. However, those who have understood the power of active listening have seen it work its magic in personal relationships, office meetings, customer service, negotiations, and even in leadership roles.

2.1. What Is Active Listening?

Active listening is a communication technique that requires the listener to fully concentrate, understand, respond, and then remember what is being said. It's much more than just hearing the spoken words. It's about understanding the message being conveyed, both from the words used and the nonverbal cues that accompany them.

While listening seems like a passive activity, when you engage in active listening, you'll find that it's a highly participative act. It involves using body language, summarizing, paraphrasing, and understanding underlying meanings. Here, the listener encourages the speaker to express their thoughts, thereby improving mutual understanding. This underscores the active element of active listening.

2.2. The Neuroscience of Listening

Research shows that active listening activates the prefrontal cortex of the brain, the area responsible for understanding the perspective of others. It triggers empathy, helps us "get in the shoes" of the speaker, and makes us more open-minded. This reduces misunderstanding and promotes more effective communication.

When you actively listen, you are not just making the speaker feel valued, you are also embedding their words, sentiments, and emotional state deeply into your memory. This result is a deeper connection between the speaker and listener, improved rapport, and the creation of a favorable environment for further communication.

2.3. Techniques of Active Listening

To practice active listening, numerous techniques can be utilized.

1. Making Eye Contact: This shows the speaker that you're paying attention and that their words are landing. It also helps you pick up on nonverbal cues, which can provide more context.

2. Utilizing Nonverbal Communication: Nodding, leaning in slightly, and adopting an open posture can show speakers that you're engaged.

3. Offering Feedback: You could summarise, paraphrase, or ask clarifying questions to demonstrate understanding.

4. Resisting Interruption: This involves refraining from jumping in with your views until the speaker has finished speaking.

5. Reflecting and Responding: This is the last step in which you reflect on what was said and respond appropriately.

2.4. Implementing Active Listening in Communication

To bring active listening to your communication, begin with the intent to understand more than to respond. Responding comes naturally, but understanding requires time, patience, and most notably, active listening.

Active listening can be especially helpful in a business environment. Imagine a negotiation or discussion scenario where you actively listen to the other party. It encourages them to express themselves entirely, thereby giving you a comprehensive understanding of their position. This understanding can aid you in crafting precise responses or solutions that are more likely to be accepted.

Active listening is also beneficial in fostering positive relationships. By providing a supportive environment and making individuals feel heard, trust and rapport are built. In a team context, this promotes collaboration, problem-solving, and innovation.

2.5. The Benefits of Active Listening

Active listening can bring a remarkable shift in your communications and relationships. Here's a list of potential benefits it brings:

1. Deepens Relationships: By creating an understanding and empathetic environment, relationships are strengthed and enhanced.

2. Improves Productivity: With less misunderstanding, teams will spend less time resolving conflicts and more time delivering results.

3. Supports Emotional Well-being: When people feel heard, it fosters an atmosphere of respect and value, which often translates into improved job satisfaction and morale.

4. Encourages Learning: By being an active listener, you expose yourself to various perspectives, which leads to broader thinking and learning.

Honing the skill of active listening might take some practice, but the results are unquestionably worth it. As you venture on this journey, remember to be patient and open-minded. Practice regularly, whether in meetings, during casual conversations or in negotiations. Soon, you'll watch as your communications transform, and doors to unimaginable possibilities open. Make active listening your secret sauce to outstanding communication. After all, when we listen effectively, we engage in a dialogue that has the potential to change lives, mend relationships, and create harmony. Happy listening!

Chapter 3. The Art of Asking Effective Questions

Communication at its heart is a process of transferring information from one party to another. While many think of speech as the primary vessel of this transmission, the act of asking questions deserves equal, if not more, credit for affirming and facilitating this exchange. Effectively inquiring can unlock the facts, feelings, thoughts, and opinions harbored deep inside the brains of our conversational counterparts.

3.1. Why Ask Questions

Understanding the importance of asking questions is step one. It accomplishes two central tasks. First, it shows you are engaged and dedicated to listening, thereby establishing rapport. Second, it allows you to procure specific information, instead of making assumptions or hoping your conversation partner will provide what you need unsolicited.

Questions enable us to delve deeper into conversations, solicit additional information, or redirect conversation paths in more compelling directions. Crucially, they allow us to challenge our own and others' presuppositions and surface unconscious biases.

3.2. Characteristics of Effective Questions

Not all questions are created equal. An effective query is direct, simple, purposeful, and probes into the underpinnings of the topic at hand. Let's dissect these qualities:

1. **Direct**: A good question is straightforward and targeted at

acquiring distinct insights. Beating around the bush with vague or indirect questions can lead to equally indeterminate results.

2. **Simple**: Keep your questions short and uncomplicated. Long-winded, multi-faceted questions can overwhelm, confuse, or frustrate the respondent.

3. **Purposeful**: An effective question serves the broader objectives of the conversation, subtly guiding the dialogue without domineering it.

4. **Probing**: Sometimes, it's important to dig slightly beneath the surface. Probing questions aim to uncover the reasons, motivations, and feelings that undergird one's responses or actions.

3.3. Categories of Questions

There are multiple kinds of questions, each best suited to a different situation. Let's enumerate some common varieties:

1. **Closed-ended**: These questions are designed to yield specific, often "yes" or "no" answers. They're useful when needing to confirm facts or make decisions.

2. **Open-ended**: These questions solicit more expansive responses, usually in the form of sentences or narratives. They're ideal for coaxing out feelings, ideas, or opinions, and engendering more nuanced discussion.

3. **Follow-up**: These questions help us collect additional information and promote deeper understanding. For example, "Can you tell me more about that?" or "What lead you to make that decision?"

4. **Reflective**: These questions mirror what the speaker has said, offering them a chance to consider their thoughts more deeply and clarify or elaborate on them. For example, "It sounds like you're saying... Is that correct?"

5. **Clarifying**: These questions are aimed at ensuring you're getting the full picture. For example, "What do you mean when you say... ?"

3.4. The Balance of Questions

Although questions are powerful tools, they must be balanced with statements and responses that demonstrate active listening. Overloading on questions can make the recipient feel like they're being interrogated. Following each question with an attentive listening and processing period allows for a more equal dialogue.

A good rhythm to adopt is to listen attentively, interject open-ended questions where necessary, provide reflecting statements to show understanding, use clarifying questions to iron out ambiguity, then resume listening attentively. Such a balance won't disrupt the flow of the conversation.

3.5. The Gentle Art of Probing

Probing is an essential art that involves asking multiple layers of questions to unearth deeper responses and perspectives. While probing, be respectful, don't interrupt, and employ open-ended questions. The purpose isn't to create discomfort, but to help the speaker think more deeply and share more insight.

3.6. Techniques for Formulating Effective Questions

How you frame your question is equally important as the content of the question itself. Some effective techniques include being specific, using neutral wording, providing an appropriate context, and keeping your queries concise. Avoid leading questions, as they coax the respondent into your desired answer rather than their genuine response. Instead, remain neutral and open to all responses.

3.7. Questions in Practice

It's all well and good to understand theoretically, but let's look at how to craft effective questions in practice.

If you're brainstorming project ideas, instead of asking 'What should we do?", try 'What problems are we facing that need attention?' or 'On which areas can we improve?'. These open-ended queries compel creative thinking and clearer objectives.

In a conflict scenario, rather than asking 'Why did you do that?', tentatively pose 'Can you help me understand your thought process?'. This respectful solicitation of perspective lessens defensiveness and promotes dialog.

Remember, there's a wealth of valuable insights laying dormant in the minds of your peers, awaiting the right question to unleash them. Master the art of asking effective questions, and you'll become an exceptional communicator, sounding board, and resolver of problems. You gain a deeper understanding of individuals, topics, and situations, and foster healthier, more productive relationships.

So, keep the information in this guide handy, and start formulating better, more effective questions to improve both your personal and professional communication.

Chapter 4. Decoding Non-Verbal Cues: Beyond Words

Every conversation has two aspects: what is spoken, and what is unspoken. This chapter will guide you through the fascinating subtleties of non-verbal communication, transforming every interaction into an opportunity for enhanced understanding and connection.

4.1. The Power of Non-Verbal Communication

Understanding others go far beyond their words. Non-verbal cues like facial expressions, body language, and tone of voice often convey more than what is spoken. Studies in communication suggest that up to 93% of our messages are transmitted non-verbally, demonstrating the power of these unspoken cues.

Non-verbal communication enables us to gauge others' feelings, attitudes, and thoughts, often before they even speak. Not only does it aid in interpreting others, but it also assists us in adjusting our responses and behavior to establish a better connection.

4.2. Decoding Facial Expressions

As the most expressive part of our body, the face reveals a multitude of emotions. A smile may convey happiness, a frown could signal worry, and raised eyebrows might reflect surprise. Investing time in understanding facial expressions can provide a more profound comprehension of the emotions surrounding a conversation.

4.3. Body Language

While faces reveal emotion, body language communicates attitudes or feelings. A person sitting erectly might be attentive and interested, fold arms could signal defensiveness, while a relaxed posture might suggest comfort and familiarity. Understanding the nuances of body language can provide a comprehensive understanding of individuals' intentions.

4.4. The Tone of Voice

The tone of voice can convey a plethora of underlying meanings. A fast-paced voice might signify nervousness or excitement, a slow tempo can exhibit calm or boredom, while fluctuations in tone might hint at the speaker's uncertainty. Listening for these voice alterations can provide a comprehensive understanding of the emotions underlying the words spoken.

4.5. Non-Verbal Communication Across Cultures

Interpreting non-verbal cues isn't universal but varies across cultures. For example, a thumbs-up is well-received in many societies but could be offensive in others. Awareness of cultural nuances is critical when decoding non-verbal cues for accurate understanding.

4.6. Eyes: The Windows to the Soul

Eyes can be a treasure trove of non-verbal information. Constant eye contact might exhibit confidence or interest, averted gaze could reflect discomfort, while frequent blinking may signal nervousness. Observing these minute changes in eye behavior can provide significant insights into a person's emotional state.

4.7. Touch: An Intimate Element

Touch, or haptics, is a potent non-verbal communicator, relaying messages of trust, understanding, and comfort. It is, however, highly subjective and should be approached with utmost subtleness.

4.8. Interpreting Silence

Silence carries a profound significance in communication. It could represent thoughtfulness, discomfort, anger, or sadness. Utilizing the power of silence effectively can transform a conversation while creating a comfortable and understanding environment for communication.

4.9. Enhancing Your Non-Verbal Communication Abilities

Decoding non-verbal cues can seem daunting at first. However, with practice and observation, you can refine your skills, enhancing your interactions in personal or professional spheres. Start by observing your non-verbal behavior and others around you, cultivating empathy and acknowledging cultural differences. Thereafter, aim to align your non-verbal signals with the words you speak for enhanced clarity in communication.

Non-verbal communication is a captivating realm that can enrich your ability to connect with others. By learning to decode these unspoken messages, you can foster empathy, build trust, and establish more meaningful personal and professional relationships.

Chapter 5. Barriers: Communication Obstacles and How to Overcome Them

Communication is a dynamic process with a myriad of factors at play that could impact its efficacy. In this portion of our guide, we'll explore various barriers that hinder effective communication and suggest strategies to overcome them.

5.1. Information Overload

One of the most common challenges impacting communication in modern times is information overload. In the hustle and bustle of the fast-paced, digitalized world, we are bombarded with information from multiple sources which could lead to confusion and misunderstandings.

To overcome this hurdle, apply the following strategies:

1. Prioritize: Not all information is equally important. Learn to differentiate between critical and non-critical information.

2. Organize: Develop a system to categorize, store, and retrieve information efficiently.

3. Filter: Use tools and software that help in filtering out unnecessary information.

5.2. Physical Noise

Environmental distractions, like background noise or an uncomfortable setting, can obstruct the transmission and reception of a message. Physical noise is detrimental to both spoken and written conversations.

Mitigation strategies include:

1. Choose a quiet environment for important discussions.

2. Use noise-cancelling headphones during video or audio conferences.

3. Make sure written communications are visually clean and free from clutter.

5.3. Emotional Barriers

Emotional barriers, like fear, mistrust, or prejudices, can cloud judgement and interpretation of messages. They can cause people to hold back and not express their thoughts completely or honestly.

Counter emotional barriers with:

1. Developing empathy towards others' perspectives.

2. Addressing personal biases and preconceived notions.

3. Cultivating a safe and open communication environment.

5.4. Lack of Active Listening

The importance of active listening in communication cannot be stressed enough. The absence of active listening can result in misinterpretation and misunderstanding of messages, breaking down the communication process.

To foster active listening:

1. Practice patience and let the speaker finish before responding.

2. Show acknowledgement by nodding or rephrasing their words.

3. Ask clarifying questions when unsure about the speaker's point.

5.5. Linguistic Barriers

Differences in languages, dialects, or industry jargon can act as roadblocks in smooth communication. Misinterpretations or misuse of language can lead to confusion or conflict.

Overcome linguistic barriers by:

1. Using simple language.

2. Explaining industry-specific terminologies.

3. Utilizing translation tools, if needed.

5.6. Cultural Differences

Cultural differences can influence communication styles and interpretations. Misunderstandings can arise due to different social norms, language nuances, or non-verbal communication styles among different cultures.

To navigate cultural differences:

1. Have an understanding of the culture you are communicating with.

2. Respect cultural norms and styles of communication.

3. Seek help from cultural advisors, if available.

5.7. Technological Challenges

The reliance on technology for communication can pose its own set of challenges. Technical issues like poor connectivity, lack of access to certain software, or hardware failure can disrupt communication.

Mitigate technological challenges by:

1. Investing in reliable communication tools and hardware.

2. Ensuring access to contingency communication channels.

3. Providing training to use digital tools effectively.

Obstacles in communication are not only common but inevitable. However, with conscious effort and effective strategies, these barriers can be mitigated, fostering smoother and more impactful communication. Remember, at the heart of successful communication lies the ability to ask, listen, and grow.

Chapter 6. Improving Listening, Enhancing Relationships

Listening is an integral tool that plays a crucial role in personal and professional relationships. Listening, truly hearing what others are saying, can increase understanding, build trust, and improve collaboration, thus enhancing relationships. Let's journey through the key aspects of active listening and the techniques that can elevate your interactions.

6.1. The Power of Listening

Before we embark to improve our listening skills, it is essential to understand why it is so vital in the first place. Whenever you interact with others, the majority of the information exchange happens through spoken words. Your ability to understand these words accurately is directly proportional to the effectiveness of these interactions. Moreover, it's not just about comprehending verbal communication; it's about gauging the undercurrents of emotions and intentions that underlie the spoken words. That's where active listening comes into play.

When you listen actively, you're not just connecting to the words or information; you connect to the speaker at a deeper, emotional level. You empathize with their sentiments, offer validation, and engage in a manner that enhances mutual respect and understanding.

There are countless examples of how active listening has salvaged relationships, brought companies back on track, and resolved complex conflicts. One of the most famous instances of recent times includes how Starbucks, under Howard Schultz's leadership, actively listened to its employees' feedback, which played a key role in turning around the company.

6.2. Understanding Active Listening

Active listening is not a passive act. It's an interactive process that demands the listener's undivided attention to both, the spoken words and unspoken emotions. This process is characteristically divided into five key stages: receiving, understanding, remembering, evaluating, and responding.

1. *Receiving*: This is the stage where you're physically hearing the speaker, and your focus determines what you receive.

2. *Understanding*: This is where you start decoding the received information, translate the words and their implications.

3. *Remembering*: As the name suggests, you retain key parts of the conversation in your memory, ensuring that the information is readily available for future reference.

4. *Evaluating*: Here, you critically assess the information, question assumptions, and analyze implications.

5. *Responding*: This is the final step where your reactions and responses reflect your understanding, evaluation, and engagement in the conversation.

To be an active listener, you must pass through each stage, ensuring you're fully engaged at every moment.

6.3. Techniques to Enhance Active Listening

Improving active listening skills requires discipline, practice, and the application of some effective techniques. Let's dive into them:

1. *Provide Undivided Attention*: Ensure that when someone is

speaking, you give them your full attention. Avoid distractions, put down your phone, and maintain eye contact with the speaker. This approach signifies respect and interest.

2. *Reflect and Clarify*: Summarize the speaker's point of view to ensure understanding, and to clarify any confusing points. It's always helpful to say, "So to clarify, you're suggesting..."

3. *Use Nonverbal Cues*: Nods, smiles, and other nonverbal cues can be potent indicators that you are engaged in the conversation. These visual signals go a long way in making the speaker feel heard.

4. *Avoid Interrupting*: Constant interruptions can be major barriers to effective communication. Practice patience and respect for the speaker's train of thought.

6.4. Active Listening and Relationships

Active listening can bring about a remarkable improvement in relationships. When you listen actively, you demonstrate empathy and understanding, fostering a closer and deeper connection with others. Both personal and professional relationships benefit equally from active listening skills.

For example, in a personal relationship, active listening allows you to understand your partner's perspectives better, avoid misunderstandings, and respond in a more thoughtful, caring manner. Professionally, active listening helps in understanding colleagues and clients better, ensuring better collaboration and stronger rapport.

6.5. Practice Makes Progress

Like any new skill, active listening requires practice. Starting might seem challenging, but with consistency, things will get easier. Implementing these techniques can begin changing your conversations, and ultimately, your relationships.

Reflect on daily interactions and note what went well and what could be improved. Encourage feedback from others about your listening skills—it helps to have external perspectives. The goal is to grow consistently, moving towards improved communication and enhanced relationships.

Listening isn't passive absorption; it's active engagement. A well-practiced skill of active listening can bridge gaps, resolve conflicts, and foster healthy relationships. Remember, communication is less about making speeches and more about active listening, understanding, and responding accurately — a skill that, once mastered, can significantly enhance your relationships.

Embarking on this journey might feel overwhelming initially, but remember: every step you take towards becoming an active listener brings you closer to having stronger, more fulfilling relationships. The impact of active listening extends far beyond the immediate conversation—it permeates your entire life, infusing all your relationships with greater understanding, empathy, and authenticity.

Improving listening and enhancing relationships is not a destination but a continuous journey. So equip yourself with these insights, commit to practicing active listening, and embark on your journey to improved communication and stronger relationships.

Chapter 7. Aiding professional growth with Active Listening

Effective communication can fuel your trajectory towards successful career growth. It bolsters your ability to work well with colleagues, manage teams, and maintain healthy interactions with clients. If communication is a two-way street, then active listening is the secret passageway that keeps this traffic flow smooth and efficient.

Active listening is not just about hearing the words that someone else is saying. Rather, it is a conscious process that demands one to understand, interpret, and derive value from the conversation. This tool consistently facilitates better understanding, stronger relationships, and, most importantly, exceptional professional growth.

7.1. The Power of Active Listening

One study after another has shown that active listeners are better leaders. They have better rapport with their team, make informed decisions, and foster a healthier work environment. By paying close attention to the other person and refraining from interrupting, they foster trust and respect.

Moreover, active listening promotes critical thinking, a crucial ingredient for decision-making. It enables you to assimilate information, analyze it, and use it to make informed choices. Active listening is therefore synonymous with enhanced comprehension and superior decision-making skills, both of which are prerequisites for professional growth.

7.2. Increasing Productivity with Active Listening

Another facet of active listening is its knack for reducing misunderstandings and preventing conflicts in the workplace. This strategy complements comprehension and ensures everyone is on the same page, thereby minimizing the chances of misunderstandings that could potentially disrupt workflow. Such a situation not only enhances team collaboration but also improves overall productivity.

While it might seem overwhelming initially, the effort is worth the reward. By dedicating an ear to your colleagues, you inadvertently create an environment where everyone is heard, opinions are respected, and arguments are healthy — a perfect blend to stimulate creativity and innovation.

7.3. Refining Leadership Qualities Through Active Listening

Active listening also contributes substantially to the development of leadership qualities. A good leader fosters rapport, understanding, and empathy among their team members. Achieving this is not possible without possessing exceptional active listening skills.

Leaders who listen actively are perceived as people-centric, a trait that sets them apart. Employees want leaders who value their inputs and take them into consideration while making decisions. In other words, active listening solidifies your reputation as an effective leader and helps you to ascend the ladder of professional growth swiftly.

7.4. Turning Feedback into Growth Opportunities

Feedback, both positive and negative, is fundamental for professional growth. Practicing active listening allows you to understand feedback in the right light, ask appropriate questions, and utilize it constructively. Rather than perceiving negative feedback as criticism, it helps transform it into opportunities for learning and growth. Similarly, positive feedback is a reinforcer to continue performing well.

Receiving feedback is just one part of the story. The other part is giving feedback - a leader should be able to provide constructive, meaningful feedback, and active listening paves the way for that.

7.5. Building Better Client Relationships Through Active Listening

Active listening transcends the boundaries of internal affairs and also comes into play while interacting with clients or negotiating deals. Showing your clients that you genuinely listen and understand their needs can make them feel important and valued. This, in turn, improves client satisfaction and ensures long-term business relationships.

In conclusion, active listening is a fantastic tool for fostering professional growth. And while incorporating active listening might be a challenge, practise makes it easier. Start by giving people your undivided attention when they are speaking, avoid interruptions, and ask open-ended questions to encourage dialogue. Be tolerant of different opinions, and respond constructively to the speaker's ideas. Remember, the journey of a thousand miles begins with one step, or in this case, with one word - Listen!

Chapter 8. Practical Exercises to Hone Your Listening Skills

The journey to becoming a better listener is highly practical; it's learned not just through theory, but by committing yourself to a collection of exercises that bolster your ability to empathize, understand, and respond effectively. These exercises are fundamental tools for sharpening your skills and turning your interaction into meaningful engagement. Let's delve right into these practical exercises designed to fine-tune your listening skills.

8.1. Exercise 1: Mindful Listening

Mindful listening is about being present in the moment and fully absorbing what is being said without succumbing to distractions or constructing a response before the speaker has finished.

So, how can you practice mindful listening? This exercise, known as "The Silent Treatment," would prove beneficial:

1. Find a quiet place and take a few deep breaths to center your focus.

2. Pick a sound in your environment – it could simply be the ticking of a clock or the hum of the refrigerator.

3. Spend a few minutes focusing solely on that sound, paying attention to its details and nuances. If your mind wanders, gently bring it back.

4. Practice this daily, increasing the listening period gradually.

The essence of this exercise is developing your ability to concentrate. You'll find that with time, you can apply the same principles during conversations.

8.2. Exercise 2: Non-Verbal Cue Detection

Communication is about more than words – it's also about reading non-verbal signals. These signals can reveal what words sometimes can't. Mastering non-verbal cues boosts your ability to really apprehend what the speaker is saying.

The "Emotion Detective" exercise can help you hone your non-verbal detection skills:

1. Choose a public place, like a park or café, where you can observe people's interactions without intruding.

2. Notice the body language, facial expressions, gestures, or any other non-verbal cues.

3. Try to deduce what emotions these people might be experiencing.

4. Compare your observations with their spoken words if you can hear them.

Practicing this exercise helps you recognize the importance of body language and non-verbal cues, allowing you unearth underlying sentiments in actual conversations.

8.3. Exercise 3: Paraphrasing For Understanding

Paraphrasing is an effective active listening technique that involves restating what the speaker has said using your own words. This demonstrates that you've understood the speaker's message and encourages clarity.

Let's practice the "Mirror Talk" exercise:

1. Engage in a conversation with a friend or colleague, asking them to tell a story or explain a concept.

2. Once they're done, paraphrase their points in your own words and ask if that aligns with their intended meaning.

3. If it doesn't, ask them to elaborate further and then try to paraphrase it again.

This continuously evolving dialogue not only promotes better understanding but also ensures that both parties are on the same page.

8.4. Exercise 4: Empathic Listening

Empathy forms the bedrock of meaningful communication. Getting under the skin of the speaker helps build a depth of understanding and makes the speaker feel valued and heard.

To enhance empathic listening, try the "Stepping into their Shoes" exercise:

1. Choose a close friend or family member.

2. Ask them to share a recent experience, preferably one that evoked strong emotions.

3. As you listen, try to genuinely understand and feel their experience. This isn't about solving their issues but about fully grasping their feelings.

This exercise helps to cultivate a deeper level of empathy and appreciation for the speaker's perspective.

8.5. Exercise 5: The Power of the Pause

Pauses in a conversation are not voids waiting to be filled; they're opportunities for reflection. Cultivating the habit of embracing silence is a valuable listening skill.

The exercise "Embracing the Silence" will help you to practice this:

1. Engage in a conversation with somebody and consciously incorporate pauses.

2. During these pauses, reflect on what has been said before formulating your response.

3. Resist the urge to immediately fill in the silence.

This method enables you to respond thoughtfully rather than impulsively, fostering deeper understanding.

Regularly practicing these exercises in your daily communications can profoundly enhance your listening skills, promoting healthier and more meaningful relationships both personally and professionally. As you master these techniques, you'll find yourself evolving into a proactive listener who can effortlessly transform any conversation into a pathway for personal and communal growth.

Chapter 9. Case Studies: Success Stories in Active Listening

The unveiling of our journey ventures into the vast world of active listening, showcasing the triumphs of those who have managed to grasp this skill par excellence, and used it to their advantage. In these fascinating tales of turning points, you will come across everyday people, professionals, and leading business magnates who mastered the art and science of listening, leading to their notable successes.

9.1. Heroes of Everyday Life

Let's start with the ordinary, everyday stories that prove just how extraordinary active listening can be. Christina is a life coach and her client, Joan, had been facing difficulties managing her work-life balance. Joan was often anxious and felt like she was failing in every role she played in her life. The pressure was overwhelming. Christina knew that she had to use the power of active listening to help Joan.

The countless hours spent patiently hearing Joan's worries, concerns, the weight she carried in her words allowed Christina to grasp the crux of Joan's problem. She was trying to be perfect in each role. Christina helped Joan realize that it's okay not to be perfect all the time and worked with her to set reasonable expectations with her husband and kids. The result turned out to be incredible. Joan found herself able to handle responsibilities better, and her overall anxiety levels plummeted.

9.2. Professionals Turning the Tide

The importance of active listening in a professional setting is equally compelling. Take, for instance, David. David was a junior partner at a law firm. He was assigned a case that had been stagnating for months due to a lack of progress. Not many believed it could be solved, but David chose to approach the situation differently. Instead of relying on the case files alone, he decided to meet the client and listen to her story.

By actively listening to his client, he understood the case from a different perspective and was able to identify that there was an overlooked piece of evidence that broke the case. David's ability to actively listen turned what seemed like an impossible case to resolve into a victory for his client.

9.3. Top-tier Executives and Listening Triumphs

The higher the level you reach in your career, the more active listening becomes a significant facet of your success. One such story is of Carina, a VP at a major tech company. She's known for her wise business decisions and has a knack for identifying the next big thing.

Earlier, her company was on the brink of making a costly mistake-pouring resources into a product that wouldn't sell. Carina suspected that her team was missing something and decided to gather feedback from multiple sources throughout the company. She started with her team, extending to other departments and down to the production team. Carina's commitment to actively listening to these diverse viewpoints allowed her to gather insights that executive reports didn't provide.

Combining these insights, Carina was able to convince the board that the proposed product was a misstep. Instead, they shifted resources to a more promising project. By practicing active listening, Carina helped her company avert an expensive failure and redirected the focus to a more successful path.

These stories are among a myriad of examples that demonstrate the remarkable power of active listening. The real-life lessons they provide are quite clear: we have much to gain when we opt to listen more actively. Beyond the boardroom, the courtroom, or the living room, active listening makes a difference. When we stop to truly hear, we open ourselves to thoughts, ideas, and perspectives that we might otherwise miss - and these often hold the keys to the solutions and successes we seek.

Chapter 10. The Science Behind Active Listening

Fundamentally, communication is about sending and receiving information. However, many interactions focus primarily on the sending, or speaking, part of conversation, and underestimate the power of listening. You, my friend, are about to step into a more nuanced understanding of this vital, yet often overlooked skill - active listening.

Active listening involves giving full attention to the speaker, absorbing, understanding the information, and responding thoughtfully. Studies show that, on average, we retain just 25% of the information we hear. With active listening, we can drastically improve this percentage. It's more than mere hearing; it's a dynamic and empathetic engagement with the speaker.

10.1. The Neurological Aspect

To comprehend the science behind active listening, let's start with how our brain responds during the process. When we listen actively, two primary regions in our brain get involved: the temporal lobes and the prefrontal cortex. The temporal lobes are responsible for processing sound, while the prefrontal cortex provides the cognitive faculties to understand and respond to the information.

In simple terms, active listening is an intense brain workout! It requires focus, processing, comprehension, memory, and empathy, engaging multiple areas of the brain simultaneously.

10.2. Emotional Intelligence and Listening

At first glance, you might not link emotions with the act of listening. However, there's a direct correlation. Active listening is tied closely to emotional intelligence—the ability to understand, use, and manage your own emotions in positive ways.

Why? Because active listening requires empathy - being able to tune into the emotions of the speaker, identify their feelings, and respond appropriately. This ability, in turn, fosters stronger, deeper connections with others, leading to more satisfying and effective interactions.

10.3. Active versus Passive Listening

Comparing active and passive listening can help us further comprehend the science behind them. When we passively listen, we're hearing the words but not necessarily engaging with the message. The auditory information makes a quick trip through the ear and into the short-term memory, where, more often than not, it quickly fades away.

In contrast, active listening invokes the process of storing audio information efficiently in our long-term memory. Active listeners are consciously seeking to understand and remember the speaker's message and will frequently paraphrase or ask follow-up questions to confirm their understanding. As you can see, even at the neurological level, active listening is more involved and interactive, fostering more profound comprehension and retention.

10.4. The Psychology of Active Listening

The psychological aspects of active listening are equally as critical as the neurological. When someone feels they're being genuinely listened to, it fulfills several potent psychological needs: validation, understanding, and respect.

Listening attentively signals to the speaker that their opinions and feelings matter. This recognition then promotes more free and open communication, fostering trust, empathy, and mutual respect—keys to any successful relationship, be it personal or professional.

Additionally, active listening helps to avoid misunderstandings and miscommunications. Individuals are less likely to become defensive or shut down when they feel their message is received accurately, leading to more productive conversations and solutions.

10.5. Misconceptions about Listening

Despite its apparent advantages, active listening is often misunderstood. Many see it as merely being silent while another talks, only to await their turn to speak. But active listening is not about silence; it's about engagement. It's an interactive process of validation, interpretation, and feedback.

Remember this – listening is not the absence of speaking; it's the presence of understanding. It requires concentration, effort, and the conscious decision to understand and value the speaker's perspective.

10.6. Applying the Science

Acknowledging the science behind active listening is one thing. Consistently applying it is another. Like any skill, it takes practice to cultivate. Start small, perhaps by focusing on understanding the speaker's emotions or paraphrasing their statements. Gradually, these practices will become more natural and have a significant impact on your communication.

Active listening has the power to transform your interactions. By understanding the science behind this skill, you can harness its power to enhance your conversation, negotiation, and leadership skills.

The journey to mastering active listening may be challenging, but remember that the benefits are manifold and rewarding. Let the science be your guide as you develop this critical communication skill. Your conversations are about to take off to a whole new level of depth, understanding, and respect.

Chapter 11. The Future of Communication: What's next for Active Listeners

As we look forward, communication is set to undergo radical transformations, making active listening more important than ever. Since this will be a pivotal part of our expressive capabilities, it's vital to grasp how it will shape the future of human connections and dialogues.

11.1. Technology and Active Listening

Long gone are the days when technology was a mere convenience. Today, it's a necessity, an integral part of our lives that continues to shape how we connect and communicate. This technological revolution, however, has presented us with an ironic conundrum. Despite having numerous platforms for communication, there are mounting concerns related to authentic connection and understanding.

In this digital era, active listening is being pushed to the periphery as robotic voices replace humanistic conversation and textual exchanges strip off non-verbal cues. But technological advancements are a double-edged sword. For instance, AI technologies are being developed to recognize emotional subtleties in conversations, facilitating enriched exchanges and adding value to active listening. Imagine a future where AI not only listens but also understands and responds in meaningful ways.

However, technology doesn't replace the need for human active listeners. Instead, it enhances this skill and makes it crucial in a world saturated with impersonal, text-based communication. True active listening bridges the gap forged by sheer technological transactional exchanges, supplementing them with empathy-inducing interactions.

11.2. The Importance of Empathy

In a rapidly evolving world, empathy is becoming an invaluable asset. Active listening, an undercurrent of empathy, is the key that unlocks the treasure trove of understanding, compassion, and connection. Emphasizing emotional intelligence, it allows us to reach beyond mere spoken words to truly interpret the sentiments and intent behind the language used.

Moreover, active listening can demystify complex ideas, promoting clear and effective communication at all levels. It eliminates misunderstandings and creates an environment conducive to cooperative problem-solving.

11.3. Active Listening in Virtual Environments

As workspaces migrate from physical to virtual environments, communication dynamics are changing. A computer screen now mediates professional conversations, reviews, and negotiations, making written and verbal communication the primary players. But how does one actively listen in such scenarios?

Active listening in virtual environments demands heightened attention to verbal cues and tonal shifts, given the absence of in-person dialogs. It requires validating emotions or insights, a process that is enabled by phrases such as "I understand" or "It makes sense." Additionally, summarizing key points, asking exploratory questions, and reciprocating with thoughtful responses are indispensable practices in the virtual communication toolbox.

With increased remote work, the role of active listeners as virtual leaders is amplified. It's no longer optional but a prerequisite for successful virtual collaboration, team-building, and improved performance outcomes.

11.4. Active Listening and global communication

As our world grows more interconnected, the need for effective cross-cultural communication is more pertinent than ever. In a diverse global society, miscommunication and misunderstanding can lead to conflict. It is here that active listening comes to the forefront as a multimodal way of understanding and navigating cultural nuances.

Adapting active listening skills to appreciate and interpret different expressive styles, speech patterns, and cultural etiquettes is the cornerstone of global communication in the future.

11.5. The Role of Education

Incorporating active listening into our educational curriculum paves the path for a proactive learning environment that nurtures an empathetic society. Incorporating this communication skill as a standard part of education allows children to value and practice reflective listening from a young age, thus setting the foundation for a future where understanding and cooperation are emphasized.

Educators can utilize technology-supported active listening exercises, giving students a wholesome perspective on its importance in multifaceted communication scenarios - be it peer discussions, understanding lectures, or decoding complex concepts.

11.6. Active Listening as Corporate DNA

As corporations evolve and adapt to the ever-changing business landscape, effective communication forms the bedrock of their success. Employees who actively listen boost team morale, enhance productivity, and foster a nurturing work environment.

By ingraining active listening into their corporate DNA, organizations pave the way for enhanced customer engagement, effective conflict resolutions, and, consequently, increased customer loyalty. Therefore, investing in active listening training could become a crucial success determinant in the business world.

In conclusion, active listening is paving the way for a future where conversations are deeper and richer. It's transforming our connection with technology, fostering empathy, redefining communication in virtual environments, bridging cultural gaps in global discussions, playing a pivotal role in education, and infusing corporate culture. By being perceptive and responsive, active listeners will redefine the essence of personal and professional communication in the future.